Student Workbook

for

Around the World in 180 Days

by

Sherrie Payne

Student Workbook for Around the World in 180 Days

Manufactured in the United States of America
Sixth Printing 2006

Published By

Apologia Educational Ministries, Inc.
Anderson, IN

Printed by

CJK
Cincinnati, OH

GOALS FOR THIS STUDY

Taking each of the seven continents, one at a time, the following areas will be studied:

GEOGRAPHY (land forms, rivers, countries & cities, climate)
HISTORY (a brief overview of the history of each continent)
RELIGION (dominant religion/s of each continent; impact of Christianity)
CULTURE (government, economics, society, thought & learning, art)
KEY PEOPLE (missionaries, historical & political figures, artists, scientists)
CURRENT EVENTS/ISSUES (political, social, religious issues)

PURPOSE FOR STUDYING WORLD HISTORY & CULTURES

As you begin this history course, it is good to think for a moment about why we should even study the life and history of other countries. For the purpose of this multi-level history study guide, there are two major reasons the author had in mind when developing this course. The first reason is: "These things happened to them as examples and were written down as warnings for us..." *(I Cor. 10:32)*. The second is summed up in the words of Jesus--"Therefore go and make disciples of all nations...teaching them to obey everything I have commanded you." *(Matt. 28:19-20)*. In other words, as citizens of this country and of this world, and as Christians, we need to be aware of **what** "*things happened*" to **whom** and **why** so that we can be properly "*warned*". And by gaining an understanding of another's culture, we can better learn how to share the gospel with any that we encounter as we "*go*" through life. The more we know and understand, the better our witness will be.

Another thing to think about: You may not even be considering leaving the United States as a missionary; however, it has become quite clear that today, God seems to be sending "*the world*" to our very doorstep. In some communities across the U.S., foreigners make up a very large part of its people. This is especially true on the West Coast, the southern Border States, and in many of the large cities. In towns with colleges or universities who usually have a certain amount of international students, there is a tremendous opportunity (responsibility?) to witness to the "*world*"! Let us, therefore, be challenged by this history course and "be diligent" to study so that you can "present yourself approved to God, a worker who does not need to be ashamed...." (II Tim. 2:15).

AFRICA

RESOURCES

TEXTBOOKS

GRADE LEVEL	TITLE	AUTHOR/ PUBLISHER
7-12	*Streams of Civilization*	Christian Liberty Press
7-12	*World Studies for Christian Schools*	Bob Jones Univ. Press
7-12	*History of the World in Christian Perspective*	A Beka Book
7-12	*World Geography in Christian Perspective*	A Beka Book
	A Glorious Age in Africa	Chu & Skinner

BOOKS OF INTEREST

4th & up	*The Slave Ship*	Sterne
4th & up	*Pyramid*	David Macaulay
4th & up	*The Pharaohs of Ancient Egypt*	Elizabeth Payne
5th & up	*Mara, Daughter of the Nile*	Eloise Jarvis MGraw
5th & up	*Journey to Jo'burg*	Naidoo
5th & up	*The Golden Goblet*	Eloise Jarvis McGraw
6th & up	*How I Found Livingstone*	Sir Henry Stanley
8th & up	*Cry, The Beloved Country*	Alan Paton
9th & up	*Heart of Darkness**	Joseph Conrad
	*(Study guide available from Progeny Press)	

MISSIONARIES TO READ ABOUT

Mary Slessor	C. T. Studd	Robert Moffat
David Livingston	Sir Henry M. Stanley	

OTHER PEOPLE YOU MAY WANT TO READ ABOUT

Cleopatra	Pharaoh Khufu (Cheops)
King Tut	Pharaoh Khafre

AFRICA: GEOGRAPHY

Use an atlas, encyclopedia, textbooks, and/or library books to find answers to the following questions.

IDENTIFY:

1. the large desert located in northern Africa -

2. the mountain range in northwestern Africa -

3. Africa's highest mountain peak -

4. Africa's largest lake -

5. the world's longest river which is located in Africa -

6. Africa's second longest river -

4

DEFINE:

1.   savanna -

2.   plateau -

3.   steppe -

4.   wadi -

5.   cataract (as along the Nile River) -

6.   delta -

7.   tropical rain forest -

8.   jungle -

9.   Bedouins -

10. cape -

GEOGRAPHY QUESTIONS:

1.   **[HS]**:   Describe the topography of Egypt. Explain the difference between "upper Egypt" and "lower Egypt".

   [UE/JH]: Explain what is meant by "upper Egypt" and "lower Egypt".

2.   Describe the climate of Egypt.

3.   Describe the climate (type of seasons) in the rest of Africa.

4.   What is the source of the Nile River?   In what country is this lake located?

5.   What is the Great Rift Valley? How long is it?

6.   In what country is Africa's highest mountain peak located?

7.   Where is "Timbuktu" located?   What is the history of this town and the meaning behind the phrase "as far away as Timbuktu"?

8.   List at least five of Africa's native animals. Also tell where each of these animals would be found (i.e., grasslands, jungles, etc.)

9.   List at least three of Africa's native plant life. Give the following information
     for each plant: 1) type of environment in which the plant is found,
                            2) uses for the plant,
                            3) any unusual description.

10. List several of Africa's natural resources.

11. **[HS]** What was the country of Zimbabwe called before 1980?

12. **[HS]** What is a possible explanation for the Atlas Mountains, the Great Rift
     Valley, and the Mediterranean Sea?   Where is the biblical reference to this
     catastrophic event?

MAP ACTIVITY. Trace a map of the continent of Africa. Label the following items.

Countries *(Capital Cities)*

___ Algeria *(Algiers)*
___ Angola *(Luanda)*
___ Benin *(Porto-Novo)*
___ Botswana *(Gaborone)*
___ Burkina Faso *(Ouagadougou)*
___ Burundi *(Bujumbura)*
___ Cabinda (belongs to Angola)
___ Cameroon *(Yaounde)*
___ Central African Republic *(Bangui)*
___ Cape Verde *(Praia)*
___ Chad *(Nidjamena)*
___ Congo *(Brazzaville)*
___ Djibouti *(Djibouti)*
___ Equatorial Guinea *(Malabo)*
___ Egypt *(Cairo)*
___ Ethiopia *(Addis Ababa)*
___ Gabon *(Libreville)*
___ The Gambia *(Banjul)*
___ Ghana *(Accra)*
___ Guinea-Bissau *(Bissau)*
___ Guinea *(Conakry)*
___ Kenya *(Nairobi)*
___ Ivory Coast *(Abidjan)*
___ Liberia *(Monrovia)*
___ Libya *(Tripoli)*
___ Mali *(Bamako)*
___ Malawi *(Lilongwe)*
___ Mauritania *(Nouakchott)*
___ Morocco *(Rabat)*
___ Mozambique *(Maputo)*
___ Namibia *(Windhoek)*
___ Niger *(Niamey)*
___ Nigeria *(Lagos)*
___ Rwanda *(Kigali)*
___ Senegal *(Dakar)*
___ Sierra Leone *(Freetown)*
___ Somalia *(Mogadishu)*
___ South Africa *(Pretoria, Capetown)*
___ Sudan *(Khartoum)*
___ Swaziland *(Mbabane)*

Lakes, Rivers, Mountains, Seas

___ Lake Victoria
___ Lake Chad
___ Lake Nasser
___ Nile River
___ Congo River
___ Niger River
___ Red Sea
___ Mediterranean Sea
___ Gulf of Aden
___ Indian Ocean
___ Atlantic Ocean
___ Atlas Mountains

Islands

___ Madagascar *(Antananarivo)*
___ Canary Islands
___ Comoros Islands

Also label:

___ the Sinai Peninsula
___ The Great Rift Valley
___ The Cape of Good Hope
___ Aswan High Dam
___ Suez Canal

Countries (Cities) cont.

___ Tanzania *(Dar es Salaam)*
___ Togo *(Lome)*
___ Tunisia *(Tunis)*
___ Uganda *(Kampala)*
___ Zaire *(Kinshasa)*
___ Zambia *(Lusaka)*
___ Zimbabwe *(Harare)*

~NOTES~

GEOGRAPHY ACTIVITY SUGGESTIONS: AFRICA

1. Memorize the capitals of several African countries. Set your own goal of how many and which ones (five countries, ten countries, all of them???)   Mark the ones you choose on the Map Activity page (page 9) with an asterisk (*).

2. Mining Africa's mineral wealth accounts for about half of the continent's total exports. The world's largest producer of gold is the area of South Africa. Find out what other major minerals are mined on this continent and where the minerals are found. Create a key and plot this on your map of Africa.

3. The Sahara Desert is growing! Research this situation and find out what is being done to slow the progress.   ✍ Write a short summary of what you find. (Suggestion: Check the Reader's Guide to Periodical Literature at your local library for magazine articles.)

4. The wild animals of Africa are world famous. Travel agencies book safaris to this mostly tropical land. Some go for the actual hunting and killing of the wild animals; others prefer doing their hunting with a camera. Suggested topics for a report are:

    [UE/JH]:   Use your imagination! Pretend you are on a safari deep in the jungles of Africa. What animals do you see? What are they doing?   ✍ Write a letter home to your family or a friend telling about your trip.   [CREATIVE WRITING]
    NOTE: If enough research is done and enough detail is included, then this could also count for SCIENCE.

    [JH/HS]:   Poaching continues to be a problem in Africa. Try to find out what is being done to limit this activity. How much of a problem is it? How much does it affect the country economically? Are some animals on the endangered species list because of poaching?   ✍ Write or tell about your findings.   [SOCIAL STUDIES/SCIENCE/SPEECH]

5. Study a product (land-use) map in an atlas. Notice how the map uses a symbol to represent the agricultural products or natural resources produced in a given area. Draw an outline map of Africa and make your own product map. Use your own symbols and make a key that explains what the symbols represent. Using colored pencils helps to make an attractive and readable map.

6. Study the time zones of the earth. Choose four different cities from this continent. Then calculate what time it is in those cities at the time you are doing this project.   [MATH]

AFRICA: HISTORY

ANCIENT HISTORY - EGYPT

Little is known about the early history of the continent of
Africa, yet one of the world's first great civilizations
developed in the northern part of this continent. The ancient
kingdom of Egypt arose along the banks of the great Nile
River. Using your textbook, atlas, library books, and encyclopedia, read about the
remarkable ancient country of Egypt. Then define the terms and answer the following
questions.

TERMS:

1.   Hieroglyphics -

2.   Papyrus -

3.   Vizier -

4.   Dynasty -

5.   Mummification -

14

STUDY QUESTIONS:

1. What benefits did the Nile River give to the ancient Egyptians?

2. Why is Egypt often called "the Gift of the Nile"?

3. What were the rulers of ancient Egypt called?

4. What major biblical person was a vizier in Egypt?

5. Why did the Egyptians build pyramids? What did this show about their religious beliefs?

6. Discuss the finding of the Rosetta Stone. (Why is it important? Who found this stone? What were they doing there?)

7. Egypt's ancient history is often referred to as having three eras -- the Old Kingdom, the Middle Kingdom, and the New Kingdom. Briefly describe each period.

~NOTES~

Suggestions for Further Research on Egyptian History:

1. Research the embalming technique the Egyptians used on their dead. ✍ Write a short summary of what you find. (SCIENCE)

2. Find out how the ancient pyramids were built.
   - 🗣 Give a "how-to" speech describing the procedure step-by-step. (SPEECH/COMPOSITION)
   - ✍ Pretend you have been hired as the architect by the pharaoh and he wants a written report from you describing how you will get the job done. (COMPOSITION--CREATIVE WRITING)

3. Find out more about hieroglyphic writing. 📄 Make a chart of a few of the characters and include their definition.

4. There was one female pharaoh. Find out what you can about Queen Hatshepsut and summarize your findings in a report. ✍

5. Read **Mara, Daughter of the Nile**. Choose a method below to report on the book.   (LITERATURE)
   - ✍ Describe Mara's personality and tell how she responded to various situations and problems she encountered.
   - 📄 Make a list of the facts you learned about ancient Egypt while reading this book.
   - ✍ Write a paragraph that describes the most exciting scene in the book.
   - ✐ Draw at least one picture from a scene in the story. (ART)
   - ✍ Write a "news brief" about the demise of Hatshepsut or Thutmose taking the throne of pharaoh.

6. 📖 King Tut is probably the one "mummy" we have all heard about. Research to find out when his tomb was found, who found it, why was he doing this search, and what he found (besides King Tut!).   Where is "King Tut" now? Give your report orally.

ANCIENT & COLONIAL HISTORY - AFRICA'S INTERIOR

As already mentioned, little is known about the ancient history of most of the continent of Africa. However, the mystery began to unfold during the world's Age of Exploration (1500s) and Africa continued to reveal more of herself, even if reluctantly, during the Colonial Era. Use your resources to find out more by defining the following terms and answering the questions.

Terms:

1.   Clan -

2.   Tribe -

3.   Oral tradition -

4.   Imperialism -

5.   Abolition -

6.   Boers -

7.   Cannibalism -

8.   Cartographer -

STUDY QUESTIONS:

1.   **[UE/JH]**   Who was the head of the tribe in early African communities?

2.   **[UE/JH]**   What function or purpose did the "witch doctor" have in the tribe?

3.   **[UE/JH]**   Why was the oral tradition so important to the early Africans?

4.   During the 19th century, serious exploration of the interior of Africa began to take place. What difficulties faced these explorers?

5.   **[HS]** Because so many explorers died during this time, what nickname became attached to Africa?

6.   Which continent was responsible for the colonization of Africa?

7.   Why were the Europeans interested in Africa? (What resources did this continent have? What did scientists find? What other kinds of information did they learn?)

8.   **[HS]** What were some of the geographic features explored and charted during the period of exploration in Africa?

9.   Who was probably Africa's greatest explorer? In what other role did he serve? When he died, what unusual thing was done with his body?

10. Who was the discoverer of Victoria Falls?

11.   Who was Henry Stanley? (What did he do? What were his famous words? What impact did David Livingstone have on Stanley?)

12.   **[HS]** Describe the situation in Africa which led to the European slave trade. (How did they get the slaves? From whom were they gathered? What was the main reason for the growth in the slave trade? Where and why was there a "need" for slavery?)

    [UE/JH] a) Why were slaves taken from Africa? Where were they taken to? b) Who sold the slaves to the European slavers? How did they get them and why did they take them?

13. Describe the conditions under which slaves were transported to their new location.

14. Where did the opposition to the slave trade begin?

15. **[JH/HS]** Why was the African country of Liberia formed?.

16.   Who was King Leopold II and what did he do that upset the other European nations?

17.   What is the "Great Trek" and why did it take place?

18.   **[UE/JH]** Why was the Boer War fought? Who won? What new country was formed at the end of this war?

19.   **[HS]** Before World War I, who controlled most of the African continent?

20.   **[HS]** What were some of the benefits of this foreign control to Africa?

21.   **[HS]** When did most of this foreign rule end?

22.   What are some of the problems and needs of modern-day Africa?

~NOTES~

<u>Suggestions for Further Research on the History of Africa:</u>

1. What is the "tsetse fly"? What impact did this fly have on Africa? (SCIENCE)

2. **[HS]** 📖 Research the practice of **apartheid** in South Africa. What is it? When did it end? What events contributed to its end? Has it been successful? Who is and what role did Nelson Mandela play in this situation?

3. **[UE/JH]** ✍ Write a paragraph about the <u>good</u> things that have come to Africa because of the Age of Exploration.

AFRICA: RELIGION

TERMS:

1.   Polytheism -

2.   Monotheism -

3.   **[HS]** Animism -

STUDY QUESTIONS:

1. **[HS]** Describe the religion of ancient Egypt.   Were they polytheistic or monotheistic?   Who were the main god/s?

    [UE/JH]   Were the ancient Egyptians polytheistic or monotheistic? Who were some of the main gods that the ancient Egyptians worshipped?

2. What did the ancient Egyptians believe happened to them after they died?

3. **[HS]**   Why did the Egyptians mummify their dead?

4.   Describe the religion of the typical African tribal community.

5.   **[UE/JH]**   What did the Africans believe about their dead ancestors?

6.   **[HS]**   What function or purpose did (does) the "witch doctor" have in the primitive tribes of Africa?

       [UE/HS]   a) Who was considered the tribal religious leader?
       b) How did this religious leader "help" people?

7.   Why were masks worn during religious ceremonies?

8.   How is tribal art reflected in their religion?

~NOTES~

<u>Suggestions for Further Research on the Religion of Africa:</u>

1. Read a biography of David Livingstone. ✍ Write a short report (one or two pages) which summarizes his life and work in Africa.

2. Read a biography of Mary Slessor. ✍ Write a short report about her which summarizes her life and work in Africa.

3. **[HS]** ☞ Research which denominations are currently the most active in evangelizing this continent. ▤ Make a poster or chart that records this information. What are the two top denominations as far as number of believers?

4. ✍ Write a letter to a missionary serving in Africa. Find out what you can about their life and work.

AFRICA: CULTURE

TERMS:

1.   Swahili -

STUDY QUESTIONS:

1.   In the tribal African culture, what is the most important group of people?

2.   Most African tribes practiced polygamy. Do you think it would be hard for the father/husband to keep peace in his family?   Why or why not?

36

3. **[HS]** How was music a part of an African's life? (When was music played or sung?   What instruments were used?)

    [UE/JH]   List some of the occasions where music would be a part of an African family's life.

4. What were the "talking drums"?   For what purposes were they used?

5. What other types of art did the Africans do?

6. What were some of the reasons that a piece of art might be made?

7. List some ways that Africans obtained their food.

~NOTES~

<u>Suggestions for Further Research on the Culture of AFRICA:</u>

1. Read about one or more of the following areas of African culture. It may be the culture of the early tribes or the culture of a modern African nation. After reading, write or tell about your findings.

    ✍ African homes   ✍ African clothing
    ✍ African food   ✍ African schools

2. ✉ Write a letter to a missionary or other person you may know about working or serving in Africa. Ask them questions about life in Africa. (What foods do they eat? How do they travel? Where do the African children go to school? What kinds of clothes do they wear? What is their house like? etc.) Share your information with a display of pictures, articles, letters, postcards, etc.

3. 📚 Choose one African nation and research its government. Who is the leader of this nation? How is he elected? What other government offices or positions are there? ✏ Draw and color the nation's flag to put with your report.

4. Pick one of the primitive African tribes and research its culture. How do they live? How do they get their food? What is their religion like? What kind of houses do they have? What roles do the men and women have? ✍ Report your information in written form or orally.

AFRICA: CURRENT EVENTS

Use the space below to record the articles you have found or the news that you have heard during your study of Africa. Clip out the news articles and glue or paste them to a separate sheet of paper. Insert those pages after this page in your notebook.

Date of Newspaper or Radio/TV Broadcast	Name of Newspaper or News Station	Topic of News Item*
_____	_____	_____
_____	_____	_____
_____	_____	_____
_____	_____	_____
_____	_____	_____
_____	_____	_____
_____	_____	_____

* Examples: National currency, war, leadership, economics, government, environment, social issues, natural disasters (earthquakes, volcano eruptions)

Australia

RESOURCES

Since Australia is not a typical part of the study of western civilization, most textbooks will not give much attention to this country. Your local library, however, will have many books that deal with the geography, history, and culture of Australia. There are also some interesting videos that can be used. (Our family enjoyed the "Five Mile Creek" video series.)

BOOKS OF INTEREST

5th up	*Walkabout*	Marshall
5th up	*Fight Against Albatross Two*	Colin Thiele
5th up	*Boy Alone*	Reginald Ottley
5th up	*The Roan Colt*	Reginald Ottley
5th up	*Rain Comes to Yamboorah*	Reginald Ottley
4th up	*Coral Reefs*	Johnson

AUSTRALIA: GEOGRAPHY

Use an atlas, encyclopedia, textbooks, and/or library books to find answers to the following questions.

IDENTIFY:

1.   the world's largest coral reef located off the coast of Australia -

2.   the world's largest single rock -

3.   the capital city of Australia -

DEFINE:

1.   dune -

2.   artesian water -

4

3.   coral reef -

4.   Aborigines -

5.   strait -

6.   basin -

7.   divide -

GEOGRAPHY QUESTIONS:

1.   What is unique about Australia as a continent?

2.   Why is Australia often called "the land down under"?

3.   To what is Australia comparable in size?

4.   What spectacular natural formation lies <u>off the northeastern coast</u> of Australia?

5.   List the three main deserts located in Australia. Also tell in which part of the continent they are located.

6.   Besides the largest single rock in the world, what other interesting things could be found if you were to visit Ayers Rock?

7. What is found in the Great Artesian Basin and what is it used for?

8. What <u>can</u> be found in Lake Eyre?   What <u>cannot</u> be found in Lake Eyre?

9. Does Australia have any mountains? If so, list them.

10. How does Tasmania differ from the other Australian states?

11. How do the seasons of Australia compare to the seasons of countries in the Northern Hemisphere?

12. What are the seasons like in Australia?

13. Which part of Australia receives the most rainfall?

14. What is the Australian "outback"?

15. List four animals that are native to Australia.

16. List two native Australian birds.

17. What two trees are native to Australia?

MAP ACTIVITY. Trace a map of the continent of Australia including its island state Tasmania. Label the following items.

States

___ New South Wales

___ South Australia

___ Western Australia

___ Northern Territory

___ Queensland

___ Victoria

___ Tasmania

Capital Cities

___ Sydney

___ Adelaide

___ Perth

___ Darwin

___ Brisbane

___ Melbourne

___ Hobart

Oceans, Seas, Rivers, Gulfs, Straits

___ Indian Ocean	___ Pacific Ocean	___ Coral Sea
___ Murray River	___ Darling River	___ Tasman Sea
___ Gulf of Carpentaria		___ Bass Strait

Mountains, Deserts, Other Landmarks

___ Great Sandy Desert	___ Gibson Desert
___ Great Victorian Desert	___ Australian Alps
___ Great Dividing Range	___ The Great Artesian Basin

The national capital city: ___ Canberra

~Notes~

GEOGRAPHY ACTIVITY SUGGESTIONS: **Australia**

1. Memorize the capitals of the seven Australian states.

2. Research to find out more about the Great Barrier Reef. What is <u>coral</u>? How large is this reef? What other sea life makes its home around the reef? ✍Record your findings. (SCIENCE)

3. Research one animal found in Australia. Write or give a report that tells about this animal's environment--where it lives, what it eats. Also, give the natural enemies of this animal and how it protects itself. How are the young cared for? When are they considered an adult? Add any other interesting information you find out. Draw or cut out a picture of this animal and add to your notebook. (LIFE SCIENCE)

4. Read about Ayers Rock. What interpretations are given by evolutionists? by creationists? ✍ Record your findings. (EARTH SCIENCE)

5. Study a product (land-use) map in an atlas. Notice how the map uses a symbol to represent the agricultural products or natural resources produced in a given area. Use the map you have already made or make another map to show your country's products. Use your own symbols and make a key that explains what the symbols represent. Using colored pencils helps to make an attractive and readable map.

Other Ideas/Notes:

AUSTRALIA: HISTORY

TERMS:

1.   squatters -

2.   Anzacs -

STUDY QUESTIONS:

1.   What are the Australian natives called?

2.   When and by whom was Australia "discovered"? What country did he
      represent?

3.   What name did he give this new land (which he claimed for his mother
      country)?

4.   What event in American history directly affected the settling of Australia?
      In what way?

5.   This new settlement eventually became what Australian city?

6.   What event in 1851 attracted a new "rush" of settlers?

7.   When did Australia become an independent nation?

8.   What type of government does Australia now have?

9.   What is the title of Australia's head of government?

10.   Who is the official head of state?

11.   What is Australia's national capital?

12.   List the major exports of Australia.

16

~Notes~

<u>Suggestions for Further Research on **Australian** History:</u>

1. Read about the Australian Aborigines. How did they handle the incoming of the British settlers? What are their customs? Where do the Aborigines live today? What is their life like now?   ✍ Give your findings in a report.

2. Draw a picture of the Australian flag. Explain its symbolism.

3. How does Australia's government differ from that of the United States? What is a <u>constitutional monarchy</u> form of government? What other nations have this type of system? Write a report or explain your answers orally to your family. [GOVERNMENT]

<u>Other Ideas/Notes:</u>

AUSTRALIA: RELIGION

Since Australia consists of two basic groups of people, the religions observed by the Australians also fall into two basic groups--the tribal beliefs of the Aborigines and various denominations of Christianity for those of British ancestry.

STUDY QUESTIONS:

1. Briefly describe the beliefs of the Aborigines who continue to practice their native religion.

2. List the most active Christian denominations of Australia in order of number of believers.

3. What is the *Uniting Church* of Australia?

~Notes~

Suggestions for Further Research on the Religion of AUSTRALIA:

1.   Find out if much missionary work is done in Australia. If so, by whom?
      What success are they having? Are there missionaries to the
      Aborigines?

Other Ideas/Notes:

AUSTRALIA: CULTURE

TERMS:

1.   Boomerang -

STUDY QUESTIONS:

1. What is the official language of Australia?

2. What is travel like for those who live in the outback?

3. How do children who live in the outback receive their education?

~Notes~

<u>Suggestions for Further Research on the Culture of AUSTRALIA:</u>

1. Read to find out some of the words unique to the Australian language. Make a list of ten or more of these words and their English (American) equivalent.

2. With the arrival of the OUTBACK® restaurants in our larger cities, we can get a taste of traditional Australian cooking. If you can't visit the restaurant, then try to find out what type of foods are typical of Australia's kitchens. Then make out a menu and describe each dish. ✍ Tell how the food was prepared (in an oven; on the "barby") as well as the main ingredients.

<u>OTHER IDEAS/NOTES:</u>

AUSTRALIA: CURRENT EVENTS

Use the space below to record the articles you have found or the news that you have heard during your study of Australia. Clip out the news articles and glue or paste them to a separate sheet of paper. Insert those pages after this page in your notebook.

Date of Newspaper or Radio/TV Broadcast	Name of Newspaper or News Station	Topic of News Item*
_____	_____	_____
_____	_____	_____
_____	_____	_____
_____	_____	_____
_____	_____	_____
_____	_____	_____
_____	_____	_____

* Examples: National currency, war, leadership, economics, government, environment, social issues, natural disasters (earthquakes, volcano eruptions)

ANTARCTICA

RESOURCES

Obviously, Antarctica is not a big topic of study in a history curriculum. Most textbooks will give only a passing mention to this continent. *National Geographic* and other magazines of this type are probably the best resource. There are also some interesting videos that can be used. Check your library.

Video: "The Big Ice"

PEOPLE YOU MAY WANT TO READ ABOUT

Richard E. Byrd   Robert F. Scott   Roald Amundsen

Antarctica: GEOGRAPHY

Use an atlas, encyclopedia, textbooks, and/or library books to find answers to the following questions.

DEFINE:

1.   ice shelf -

2.   ice floes -

3.   icebergs -

4.   krill -

5.   calving -

GEOGRAPHY QUESTIONS:

1. To what can Antarctica be compared for size?

2. At which pole is Antarctica located?

3. Describe the climate of this continent. What is the range in temperature from the coldest to the warmest?

4. Are there any mountains on Antarctica?   What are they called?

5. Give the names of some of the ice shelves that are part of this continent.

6. Is the ice on Antarctica from salt water or fresh water?

7.   Does this continent have any cities or towns?

8.   Do people visit or work on Antarctica?

9.   Where do these people stay and what do they do?

10.   List the natural resources of Antarctica.

11.   What animals can be found on Antarctica?

12.   Can any vegetation be found there?   If so, what kind?

6

~ Notes ~

MAP ACTIVITY. Trace a map of the continent of Antarctica. Label the following items.

Stations

____ Little America (USA)

____ Scott   (New Zealand)

____ McMurdo (USA)

____ Amundsen-Scott (USA)

____ Wilkes (Australia) *Casey*

____ Vostok   (Russia)

Areas

____ Marie Byrd Land

____ Victoria Land

____ Queen Maud Land

____ Antarctic Peninsula

____ Ross Ice Shelf

____ Ronne Ice Shelf

Oceans, Seas, Rivers

____ Pacific Ocean

____ Atlantic Ocean

____ Weddell Sea

____ Indian Ocean

____ Amundsen Sea

Other Landmarks

____ Transantarctic Mountains

____ Arctic Circle

Antarctic Circle

____ South Pole

GEOGRAPHY ACTIVITY SUGGESTIONS: **Antarctica**

1. Try to find the meaning of the name "Antarctica". Why was it given this name?

2. Research the tiny krill. Why is this little sea creature so important to the survival of every other animal that makes Antarctica its home.

Antarctica: HISTORY

STUDY QUESTIONS:

1.   List three early explorers and the countries they were from who were
      searching for this "unknown last continent"?   (They may not have actually
      sighted land.)

2.   Who were the two men who lead the "Great Race" to the South Pole?   What
      year did this take place?

3.   Briefly describe this race. Who won and by how long?

4. Who was the first man to fly over the South Pole?   What country was he from?

5. Who has claim or control of this continent?

6. When was this determined?   What was this agreement called?

7. Why were stations set up in Antarctica in the late 1950s?

8. What was the international organization that led to these stations being established? How many countries first participated?

9. List the three main American stations located on Antarctica.

10. What kinds of fossils have been found on this continent?

11. What are some of today's concerns regarding Antarctica?

~ Notes ~

<u>Suggestions for Further Research on **Antarctica's History:**</u>

1. Read one magazine article that deals with Antarctica.   ✍ Summarize the article. Include the name and date of the magazine with your report.

2. Read about the "Great Race" to the South Pole. Compare the number of assistants each man took with him, the number of animals used to pull the sleds, the types of provisions carried. Find out whether both teams made it safely back to their starting point.   ✍Give an oral or written report on your findings.   ▦   Or, make a poster that compares the two teams.

3. There is much in the news about the thinning of the ozone layer located over Antarctica. Is there really a "hole" in the ozone layer? What are some of the theories presented by scientists today?   ✍Report your findings.

Antarctica: CURRENT EVENTS

Use the space below to record the articles you have found or the news that you have heard during your study of Antarctica. Clip out the news articles and glue or paste them to a separate sheet of paper. Insert those pages after this page in your notebook.

Date of Newspaper or Radio/TV Broadcast	Name of Newspaper or News Station	Topic of News Item*
_____	_____	_____
_____	_____	_____
_____	_____	_____
_____	_____	_____
_____	_____	_____
_____	_____	_____
_____	_____	_____

* Examples: National currency, war, leadership, economics, government, environment, social issues, natural disasters (earthquakes, volcano eruptions))

SOUTH AMERICA

RESOURCES

TEXTBOOKS

GRADE LEVEL	TITLE	AUTHOR/ PUBLISHER
4-6	*New World History and Geography*	A Beka Book
7-12	*History of the World* in Christian Perspective	A Beka Book
7-12	*World Geography* in Christian Perspective	A Beka Book
7-12	*World Studies for Christian Schools*	Bob Jones Univ. Press

BOOKS OF INTEREST/READERS

4-6	*The Secret of the Andes*	Clark
4th up	*Chucaro; Wild Pony of the Pampa*	Kalnay
4th up	*Out on the Pampas*	G. A. Henty
5th up	*Bruchko*	Bruce Olson
5th up	*Walk the World's Rim*	Baker
5th up	*The Panama Canal*	Stein
5th up	*Through Gates of Splendor*	Elliott
6th up	*Kon-Tiki*	Heyerdahl

OTHER PEOPLE YOU MAY WANT TO READ ABOUT

Simon Bolivar   Jose de San Martin

SOUTH AMERICA: GEOGRAPHY

Use an atlas, encyclopedia, textbooks, and/or library books to find answers to the following questions.

IDENTIFY:

1.   the mountain range which runs along the western coast of South America -

2.   the tallest mountain in the western hemisphere and where it's located -

3.   the water falls which has the longest drop of any in the world and where it is located -

4

DEFINE:

1.　isthmus -

2.　mountain range -

3.　island -

4.　rain forest -

5.　sea -

6.　pampas -

GEOGRAPHY QUESTIONS:

1. List the areas (not countries) that are included in the South American continent.

2. In which hemisphere is South America located?

3. South America is the fourth largest continent. What are the three larger continents?

4. The world's largest rain forest is located on this continent. Where is this forest located?

5. What is the name of the desert located in northern Chile?

6. Which three South American countries are largely made up of rolling grasslands?

7.   The isthmus of Panama links Central America with South America at what country?

8.   List several of South America's native animals and describe any unusual characteristics as well as its natural habitat.

9.   List several plants native to South America.

10.   What major islands or island groups are part of South America?

~Notes~

MAP ACTIVITY. Trace a map of the continent of Latin (South) America. Label the following items.

Countries & Islands *(Capital Cities)*

____ Colombia *(Bogota)*

____ Argentina *(Buenos Aires)*

____ Guyana *(Georgetown)*

____ Suriname *(Paramaribo)*

____ Brazil *(Brasilia* - also show: *Sao Paulo, Rio de Janeiro)*

____ Bolivia *(La Paz)*

____ Uruguay *(Montevideo)*

____ Panama *(Panama)*

____ Nicaragua *(Managua)*

____ Guatemala *(Guatemala)*

____ Belize *(Belmopan)*

____ Cuba *(Havana)*

____ Haiti *(Port au Prince)*

____ Dominican Republic *(Santo Domingo)*

____ Grand Cayman

____ Martinique

____ Guadeloupe

____ Netherlands Antilles

____ Saint Vincent

____ Antigua

____ Tierra del Fuego

____ Peru *(Lima)*

____ Ecuador *(Quito)*

____ Venezuela *(Caracas)*

____ French Guiana *(Cayenne)*

____ Panama *(Panama)*

____ Paraguay *(Asuncion)*

____ Chile *(Santiago)*

____ Costa Rica *(San Jose)*

____ Honduras *(Tegucigalpa)*

____ El Salvador *(San Salvador)*

____ Mexico *(Mexico D. F.)*

____ Bahamas *(Nassau)*

____ Jamaica *(Kingston)*

____ Puerto Rico *(San Juan)*

____ Dominica

____ Barbados

____ Saint Lucia

____ St. Kitts

____ Grenada

____ Galapagos Islands

____ Cape Horn

Oceans, Seas, Rivers, Gulfs, Straits

____ Caribbean Sea   ____ Pacific Ocean   ____ Atlantic Ocean

____ Gulf of Mexico   ____ Strait of Magellan   ____ Panama Canal

____ Amazon River   ____ Orinoco River   ____ Uruguay River

____ Sao Francisco River

Mountains, Deserts, Other Landmarks

____ Andes Mountains   ____ Atacama Desert

____ Sierra Madres Oriental Mountains   ____ Baja California

____ Sierra Madres Occidental Mountains   ____ the equator

____ Tropic of Cancer   ____ Tropic of Capricorn

GEOGRAPHY ACTIVITY SUGGESTIONS: **SOUTH AMERICA:**

1. Memorize the capitals of several or all of the South American countries.

2. ☙ ✍ Research to find out more about the rain forests of South America. What is the economic importance of this area? Record your findings. (SCIENCE)

3. ☙ ✍ Research one animal found in South America. Write or give a report that tells about this animal's environment--where it lives, what it eats. Also, give the natural enemies of this animal and how it protects itself. How are the young cared for? When are they considered an adult? Add any other interesting information you find out. Draw or cut out a picture of this animal and add to your notebook. (LIFE SCIENCE)

4. ✍ Study a product (land-use) map in an atlas. Notice how the map uses a symbol to represent the agricultural products or natural resources produced in a given area. Draw an outline map of South America. Then use your own symbols and make a key that explains what the symbols represent. Using colored pencils helps to make an attractive and readable map.

Other Ideas/Notes:

SOUTH AMERICA: HISTORY

TERMS:

1. Iberians -

2. viceroys -

3. Creoles -

4. Caudillos -

5.   hacienda -

6.   mestizos -

7.   mulattos -

8.   conquistador -

STUDY QUESTIONS:

1.   The word "Indians" refers to what group of people in South America?

2.   What were the three main Indian groups on this continent before the European explorers arrived?

3.   Which nation was responsible for conquering the great Indian nations of South America?

4.   Who was the Inca leader at the time of the conquest by the Europeans?

5.   Who led the conquering of the Inca Indians?

6.   Which tribe controlled the Valley of Mexico and the area surrounding it?

7.   What was the name of the Aztec capital?

What is the present-day name for this area?

8.   Who was the leader of the Aztecs when the Europeans first arrived in this area?

9.   Which European leader conquered the Aztecs?

10.   Besides his own men, who also helped in him in the conquering?

11.   Why did the Aztecs not oppose the European conquerors?

12.   What group of Indians in southern Chile was able to resist being conquered for over 300 years?

13.   Besides being killed in battles, what was another reason for the decline in the Indian population after European colonists arrived in Latin America?

14.   Of the four major European countries that had the greatest number of people settling in the New World, which two of these countries focused mostly on the southern continent?

15.   Why is this area often referred to as "Latin America"?

16.   What was one major reason Europeans came to the New World?

17.	What did South America have more of than North America?

18.	Which church group took hold in Latin America?

19.	Which area in South America was controlled by the Portuguese government?

20.	Why was an imaginary line drawn, which ran north and south, through South America? What was this line called?

21.	Who were the two men who led revolutions to gain independence for South America from its European rulers?

- Notes -

<u>Suggestions for Further Research on SOUTH AMERICAN History:</u>

1. ☙ Read about life on a hacienda during the settlement period of South America. How did this compare or contrast with life in a medieval European castle.

2. Describe the problems that the Latin American countries faced as they tried to rule themselves. How has this carried through even until today?

3. Make a time line of the important historical events of this continent. Some points to include would be:
    - Peak of Mayan Indian civilization
    - Peak of Aztec Indians empire
    - Peak of Inca Indian empire
    - Christopher Columbus-- first European to reach Latin America
    - Magellan rounds the tip of South America through the strait that now bears his name
    - Spanish conquest of the major Indian civilizations completed
    - Most Latin American colonies gain their independence

4. What is a **bola**? How and for what purpose was this used by the Indians?

5. ☙ ✍ The United States was not the only nation who had to fight to gain its freedom from European control after the New World was discovered. Read about the fight for freedom of Mexico, the other Central American countries, Brazil, or the other South American countries. Choose one area and write two to four paragraphs which briefly tell when the independence was gained, who led the fight, and how the independence was finally obtained.

Other Ideas/Notes:

South America: RELIGION

STUDY QUESTIONS:

1. **[HS]** The encyclopedia says that most Latin Americans are "Christians". What do they mean by that statement?

2. **[UE/JH]** Which denomination or church do the majority of Latin Americans belong to?

3. **[UE/JH]** Do the people of Latin America have the freedom to worship as they choose?

4. **[UE/JH]** Do some governments in Latin America officially support a particular church? If so, which one?

5.   What percentage of the people are considered to be Protestant?

6.   Name some of the most active Protestant denominations in Latin America.

7.   Which two church groups have the fastest growing membership today in Latin America?

- Notes -

<u>Suggestions for Further Research on the Religion of SOUTH AMERICA:</u>

1.   ▣ Many churches support missionaries who are working in Latin America. Try to make contact with one and ask them about their work, such as: What is your biggest challenge in reaching these people? Are the people receptive to your message? What types of outreach seem to work best? Do you have churches in villages or are they in large cities?

2.   The Mormons are one of the largest churches in Latin America. Research to find out why this church seems to have a foothold in this area.

<u>Other Ideas/Notes:</u>

SOUTH AMERICA: CULTURE

TERMS:

1.   poncho -

2.   gauchos -

3.   tortilla -

4.   hacienda -

5.   fiesta -

STUDY QUESTIONS:

1.   Describe some of the typical foods that would be eaten in South America.

2.   What forms of recreation are enjoyed by the people of South American?

3.   Discuss the educational system of South America. Are most Latin Americans literate?

- Notes -

Suggestions for Further Research on the Culture of SOUTH AMERICA:

1. ♪ What are the traditional instruments used in Latin American music? What are "mariachis"? Try to find where the following music styles originated from: *samba, calypso, bossa nova*.

2. Latin American dancing is also well-known. Some steps which originated in Latin America are taught in North American ballroom dance classes. Try to identify these dances.

3. The extended family is very important in Latin American culture. If you read the book *Bruchko*, by Bruce Olson, notice what Olson points out about family life in a Motilone Indian tribe. Share your insights with your family.

OTHER IDEAS/NOTES:

SOUTH AMERICA: CURRENT EVENTS

Use the space below to record the articles you have found or the news that you have heard during your study of South America. Clip out the news articles and glue or paste them to a separate sheet of paper. Insert those pages after this page in your notebook.

Date of Newspaper or Radio/TV Broadcast	Name of Newspaper or News Station	Topic of News Item*
_____	_____	_____
_____	_____	_____
_____	_____	_____
_____	_____	_____
_____	_____	_____
_____	_____	_____
_____	_____	_____

* Examples: National currency, war, leadership, economics, government, environment, social issues, natural disasters (earthquakes, volcano eruptions)

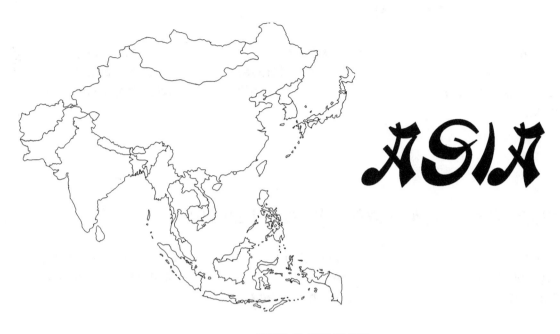

RESOURCES

TEXTBOOKS

GRADE LEVEL	TITLE	AUTHOR/ PUBLISHER
4-6	*Old World History and Geography*	A Beka Book
7-12	*History of the World in Christian Perspective*	A Beka Book
7-12	*World Geography in Christian Perspective*	A Beka Book
7-12	*World Studies for Christian Schools*	Bob Jones Univ. Press

BOOKS OF INTEREST/READERS

4th up	*The Big Wave*	Pearl S. Buck
5th up	*Commodore Perry in the Land of the Shogun*	Blumberg
5th up	*The Mogols*	Nicholson
5th up	*Tales of a Korean Grandmother*	Carpenter
5th up	*Li Lun, Lad of Courage*	Treffinger
5th up	*Ali and the Golden Eagle*	Grover
5th up	*The Samurai's Tale*	Haugaard
6th up	*The Endless Steppe*	Hautzig
6th up	*The Bronze Bow*	Speare
7th up	*The Good Earth*	Buck

MISSIONARIES TO READ ABOUT

Brother Andrew
J. Hudson Taylor
John and Betty Stam
Robert Morrison

Mother Teresa
Amy Carmichael
Jonathan Goforth

William Carey
Hannah Marshman
Adoniram Judson

OTHER PEOPLE YOU MAY WANT TO READ ABOUT

Genghis Kahn
Chiang Kai-shek
Mao Tse-tung

Kublai Khan
Marco Polo
Peter the Great

Commodore Perry
Mahatma Ghandi

ASIA: GEOGRAPHY

Use an atlas, encyclopedia, textbooks, and/or library books to find answers to the following questions.

IDENTIFY:

1.   the largest continent on earth -

2.   the highest place on earth -

3.   the lowest place on earth -

4.   the two most populous countries in the world -

5.   the large desert located in China -

6.   the highest mountain in Japan -

7.   the basic unit of Japanese currency -

8.   the two largest cities in China -

9.   the island which lies off the southern tip of India -

10.   the largest sea -

11.   the warmest ocean -

12.   the largest peninsula -

13.   the world's deepest (fresh water) lake -

14.   the world's greatest archipelago -

15.   the world's largest inland sea -

16.   the world's longest wall -

DEFINE:

1.   monsoon -

2.   tundra -

3.   alluvial plain -

4.   plateau -

5.   valley -

6.   archipelago -

7.   delta -

GEOGRAPHY QUESTIONS:

1.   List the three great fertile river valleys of Asia which were the homes of three important ancient civilizations.

2.   Because Asia is connected to the same land mass as Europe, these two continents together are sometimes called what?

3.   Asia has more mountains than any of the other continents. What benefits and what problems do these mountains cause the people of Asia?

5.   In which country (or region) can the giant panda be found?

6. Elephants are found in both Africa and Asia, yet an African elephant is different from an Asian elephant. List some of the differences.

7. Japan is made up of how many large islands and how many small islands?

8. Give the names of the four major islands.

9. Describe the landform of most of Japan. What makes it that way?

10. What is the capital city of Japan?

11. What is the average number of earthquakes per year in Japan?

12. How many volcanoes are located on the Japanese islands?

How many are active?

13. Briefly describe the climate of Japan.

14. By what name is the area in northeastern China often known?

15. By what name is the area in northwestern China often known?

16.　How did the Yellow River earn the name of "China's Sorrow"?

17.　Why is India called a "subcontinent"?

18.　List the three geographic regions that India can be divided into.

19.　List three important river systems that water the Northern Plains.

20. List some of the wildlife that is native to India.

21. What is India's basic unit of currency?

12

NOTES

MAP ACTIVITY. Trace a map of the continent of Asia. Label the following items.

Countries *(Capital Cities)*

✓ Afghanistan *(Kabul)*

✓ Bangladesh *(Dacca)*

✓ Bhutan *(Thimphu)*

✓ Myanmar ~~Burma~~ *(Rangoon)*

✓ Cambodia *(Phnom Penh)*

✓ China *(Beijing)*

✓ India *(New Delhi* also show: Calcutta, Bombay*)*

✓ Yemen Arab Republic *(San'a')*

✓ Iran *(Tehran)*

✓ Iraq *(Baghdad)*

✓ Israel *(Jerusalem)*

✓ Japan *(Tokyo)*

✓ Jordan *(Amman)*

✓ Kuwait

✓ Laos *(Vientiane)*

___ Lebanon *(Beirut)*

✓ Malaysia *(Kuala Lumpur)*

✓ Vietnam *(Hanoi, Ho Chi Minh City)*

✓ Mongolia *(Ulan Bator)*

✓ Nepal *(Kathmandu)*

✓ N. Korea *(Pyongyang)*

✓ S. Korea *(Seoul)*

✓ Oman *(Muscat)*

✓ Pakistan *(Islamabad)*

✓ Philippines *(Manila)*

✓ Qatar *(Doha)*

✓ Saudi Arabia *(Riyadh)*

✓ Singapore

✓ Sri Lanka *(Colombo)*

✓ Syria *(Damascus)*

___ Taiwan *(Taipei)* NOT a country

✓ Thailand *(Bangkok)*

✓ Turkey *(Ankara)*

___ Maldives *(Male)*

✓ Bahrain *(Manama)*

✓ United Arab Emirates *(Abu Dhabi)*

✓ Armenia

✓ Azerbaijan

___ Bahrain

✓ Brunei

✓ Cyprus

___ East Timor

✓ Georgia

✓ Indonesia

✓ Kazakhstan

✓ Kyrgyzstan

✓ Russia

✓ Tajikistan

✓ Turkmenistan

✓ Uzbekistan

Oceans, Seas, Rivers, Gulfs, Straits

___ East China Sea

___ South China Sea

___ Philippine Sea

___ Bay of Bengal

pronun ___ Sea of Okhotsk

___ Bering Strait

___ Indus River

→ ___ Ob River

___ Lake Baykal

___ Pacific Ocean

___ East China Sea

___ Sea of Japan

___ Red Sea

___ Persian Gulf

→ ___ Huang He River *(Yellow)*

___ Yangtze River

→ ___ Ural River

___ Arabian Sea

___ Yellow Sea

___ Black Sea

___ Caspian Sea

___ Gulf of Aden

___ Ganges River

→ ___ Lena River

___ Dead Sea

Mountains, Deserts, Other Landmarks

___ Himalayan Mountains

→ ___ Siberia

___ Gobi Desert

→ ___ the equator

___ Ural Mountains

___ Mt. Fujiyama ←

GEOGRAPHY ACTIVITY SUGGESTIONS: *ASIA*

1. Memorize the capitals of several Asian countries.

2. 📖✏ What is the "Ring of Fire"? What does this have to do with the number of earthquakes and volcanoes in Japan? Research and report what you find. (EARTH SCIENCE)

3. 📖✏ Research one animal found in Asia. Write or give a report that tells about this animal's environment--where it lives, what it eats. Also, give the natural enemies of this animal and how it protects itself. How are the young cared for? When are they considered an adult? Add any other interesting information that you find. Draw or cut out a picture of this animal and add to your notebook.   (LIFE SCIENCE)

4. 📖 Read to find out more about the monsoons of eastern Asia. How do they affect the climate of this area? When is the rainy season? Do monsoons only carry warm, moist air? How much rain will an area get during the monsoon season? Report what you find--either in writing or orally.   [EARTH SCIENCE]

5. ✏ Study a product (land-use) map in an atlas. Notice how the map uses a symbol to represent the agricultural products or natural resources produced in a given area. Draw an outline map of Asia to make your own product map. Use your own symbols and make a key that explains what the symbols represent. Using colored pencils helps to make an attractive and readable map.

6. Study the time zones of the earth. Choose four different cities from this continent. Then calculate what time it is in those cities at the time you are doing this project. [MATH]

7. **[UE/JH]** 📖 What happens when an earthquake occurs under water? Look up the word **tsunami** and find out why an ocean earthquake can be as destructive and deadly as one that happens on land.
    [EARTH SCIENCE]

8.   **[UE/JH]**   ▤ Most of the subcontinent of India has three seasons. Find out what these three seasons are, then make a chart which describes each season. Share the information with your family.

9.   **[UE/JH]**   ✐ Choose four nations from the continent of Asia. Draw and color their flags, state the name of each country's current political leader, list the major exports of each nation, and the nation's unit of currency. Put this information in your notebook.

Other Ideas/Notes:

ASIA: HISTORY

TERMS:

1.   dynasty -

2.   porcelain -

3.   calligraphy -

4.   kowtow -

5.   opium -

18

STUDY QUESTIONS:]

1. The Chang (Shang) dynasty was the first of around ten major dynasties in China's history. How long did this family rule?

2. For what artistic skill were the artisans of the Chang dynasty known?

3. What metals make up "bronze"?

4. The family that ruled after the Chang family had the longest rule in China's history. Which family was it?

5. How long was their rule?

6.   China experienced her "Classical Age" during this family's rule. What makes something "classic"? What does a nation's "Classical Age" offer to later generations?

7.   After the Chou dynasty collapsed, the **Ch'in** family took control. What two lasting "monuments" are left from this dynasty.

8.   The next empire was ruled by the **Han** family. List some of the achievements of China during this dynasty.

9.   What was the "Silk Road"?

10.   During the Medieval Period (beginning AD 500), the Sui, T'ang, and Sung dynasties ruled. During the T'ang and Sung dynasties, China reached her **Golden Age**. What determines a culture's Golden Age?

11.   What group of people was the most honored by the time China entered her Golden Age?

12. What made a person a "scholar" in China during this time?

13. What types of jobs would these scholars likely have?

14. China had two major periods of trading. The first was during the Han dynasty. The second was during the Yuan dynasty (1279-1368). What items did the other countries want from China?

15. What items did China want from the European world?

16. What religion entered China during this period of extensive trading?

17.   What other two religions still remained strong?

18.   The Chinese were the ones who learned how to make paper. During the Golden Age, they invented something else which enabled them to have many books and libraries. What was this?

19.   Name two other inventions that came from the Chinese.

20.   What dynasty ruled from the late 1300s to 1600s?

21.   Which dynasty was in control from 1644 until 1911?

22.   What was the Ming and Manchu dynasty's attitude toward China's trade with the outside world?

23. For the little trade that was allowed, which nation controlled most of this trading?

24. What one product did the British finally find that the Chinese wanted?

25. After the Opium Wars between China and Great Britain, treaties were signed and trade opened up again between China and the western world. This also opened the door for missionary work. Name two missionaries who spent time in China during this time.

26. **[HS]** The influx of trade with the western world caused one group of Chinese to rebel and revolt violently. This group of Chinese was called the **Boxers**. Who were they? Who and what did they adamantly oppose?

27.   **[HS]** What was one of the results of the Boxer Rebellion?

28.   What was the previous name of the country of Taiwan?

By what other name is Taiwan called?

29.   What land is nicknamed the "Land of the Rising Sun"?

30.   What name did Marco Polo give to the island country of Japan?

31. From around 1200 until the middle 1800s, Japan was a feudal aristocratic society. However, instead of kings, knights, and serfs (as in Europe), Japan had a **Mikado, shoguns, daimios, and samurais.** Define each of these roles.

32. What was Japan's ambition that led to their part in World War II?

33. What American naval base did Japan attack which led to the United States entering World War II?

34. What Japanese cities were the targets of the first two atomic bombs to be used in warfare?

35.   After World War II, what happened to the nation of Korea?

36.   What happened in 1950 which caused the Korean War?

37.   What was the result of the Korean War?

38.   **[HS]** When did Hong Kong revert to a Chinese Island? Who previously had a "mandate" on this area?

NOTES

Suggestions for Further Research on ASIAN History:

1. Find out more about China's Classical Age. Listed below are several areas influenced by this era. Briefly describe the "classical" way each was handled.

   Chinese Classical Thought
   Chinese Classical Education   *(Note: This information can be found*
   Chinese Classical Rule   *in Bob Jones' World Studies textbook,*
   Chinese Classical Families   *Chapters 5 & 9)*
   Chinese Classical Art

2. Make a time line of the important historical events of this continent. Some points to include would be:

   - Buddha is born
   - Mohammed is born
   - Confucius is born
   - Japan closes its doors to European influence and trade
   - War between China and Great Britain
   - Japan and China at War
   - World War I
   - World War II
   - Vietnam War
   - Chinese Communists conquer mainland China
   - Korean War
   - Civil War in Pakistan; Bangladesh becomes an independent
        nation

3. ☙ Find out more about the opium trade between China and Great Britain. Why were measures finally taken to stop the trade? What affect did this drug have on the Chinese people? How did the British react to the ban on trade? What war was finally fought between these two nations over this drug?

4. During the 1800s when the struggle to have open trade with China was occurring, the Europeans were competing for "spheres of influence". What does this mean? What stopped this from happening?

5. 🕮 ✍ The Manchus (Ch'ing Dynasty) were the last ruling dynasty, lasting until 1912. The Boxer Rebellion of 1899 was the "beginning of the end" for the traditional Chinese culture. Research this event and write a report which summarizes the events which followed leading up to the end of the dynasty era.

6. 🕮 ✍ The continent of Asia contains what is called the "Cradle of Civilization". All the early civilizations have their birth on this continent. Research one or two of these earliest civilizations. List their more notable achievements and report your findings. (Suggested civilizations: Sumerians, Hittites, Phoenicians, Babylonians)

7. **[HS]** Trace the history of China's governments from the collapse of the ancient dynasty system (in 1912) to the present. Include the names of the one/s in power, the type of government, and the effect on the Chinese society.

8. **[UE-HS]** 🕮 ✍ Japan shut itself off from the world for 200 years (from the 1600s to the 1800s). Why did they do this? What were the circumstances surrounding its opening up to the outside world again? Give the names of significant people involved. Write a short report on this topic and insert in your notebook.

9. **[HS]** During 1997, Hong Kong was a major news topic. Find out why. Then collect news clippings (by making copies of library resources) and write a summary of Hong Kong's past, present, and predicted political situation. ✍ Place this information in your notebook.

10. **[HS]** 🕮 Israel became a nation again in 1948. Trace the path that Israel took in order to re-establish itself as a nation. How has Israel been received by her neighboring countries? List the major wars/conflicts Israel has had with her Arab neighbors. How is this a part of the seemingly constant turmoil in the Middle East today?

Other Ideas/Notes:

ASIA: RELIGION

TERMS

1. theocracy -

2. Koran -

3. reincarnation -

4. Muslim -

5.   monotheism -

6.   guru -

7.   animism -

8.   Brahman -

STUDY QUESTIONS:

1.   Explain the school of thought called **Taoism.**

2.   Who is considered the "Father of Modern Missions"? What was his motto?

3.   What is the "law of the karma" of the Hindu faith?

✍ NOTES

Suggestions for Further Research on the Religions of *ASIA*:

1. ⌨ Many churches support missionaries who are working in Asia. Try to make contact with one and ask them about their work, such as: What is your biggest challenge in reaching these people? Are the people receptive to your message? What types of outreach seem to work best? Do you have churches in villages or are they in large cities?

2. 📖 ✍ All the world's major religions have their beginnings in Asia. For each of these major religions (excluding Christianity and Judaism), write a paragraph which summarizes the main beliefs. Include the name of the god worshipped, what is believed about life after death, any rituals that must be performed, and what is upheld as a devout lifestyle. Also tell where (in which countries) each religion is the strongest. The religions to research are:

BUDDHISM	CONFUCIANISM
HINDUISM	ISLAM
SHINTO	TAOISM

3. **[JH/HS]** ✍ Even Christianity and Judaism began in Asia. Which of the above religions has a type of "kinship" with Judaism? In what way? How is this "sibling rivalry" still an issue even today? Write a report that discusses this issue. Use current events to support your answer.

4. Christianity is the one major world religion that does not have a foothold in most parts of Asia. Why do you think this is so? Mission workers even have a term for the area where their mission efforts have been so challenging. This area is called the "**10-40 Window**". Try to find out why this term is used. (Hint: It has something to do with latitude and longitude.)

36

<u>Other Ideas/Notes:</u>

𝒜𝒮ℐ𝒜: CULTURE

TERMS:

1.   cuneiform -

2.   ziggurat -

3.   rickshaw -

4.   Yiddish -

5.   suttee -

6.   pyre -

7.   kibbutz -

8.   sari -

9.   Sanskrit -

10.   calico -

11.   kimono -

12.   pagoda -

STUDY QUESTIONS:

1.   What type of painting was the most important during China's Golden Age?

2.   Explain how a Chinese artist (during the Golden Age) would go about painting a landscape picture.

3.   Why did the Chinese build their houses long and low?

4.   Who invented the rickshaw? What circumstances surrounded this invention?

5.　　What is the system called which separates India's people into strict class divisions? Explain the divisions.

6.　　What is the **Taj Majal**? Where is it and why was it built?

7.　　What contributions has India made to world progress?

42

NOTES

<u>Suggestions for Further Research on the Culture of *ASIA*</u>

1. One can't think of Asia without thinking of rice. When most of us picture someone from the Orient we often think of someone standing in a rice paddy. Research how rice is grown. How is it planted? How long does it take to reach maturity? What kind of soil does it need? Report your findings in writing or orally. Add pictures to your report if you can.

2. Research the caste system of India. What are the main social divisions? What are the "rules" of this system? What is an "out-caste"? Include this information as well as any other interesting facts in a report. Share your information with your family and put your findings in your notebook.

3. **[HS]** Rural life in Israel differs greatly from that of other Asian nations. Find out what you can about what life would be like on an Israeli kibbutz. Explain how land ownership and labor are shared. Write a short descriptive report for your notebook.

4. **[JH/HS]** For a period in India's history, Britain controlled this nation. There were several benefits to India during this time. Research and report what these benefits were.

5. During India's struggle for independence in the early 1900s, two leaders of special note were Mahatma Gandhi and Jawaharlal Nehru. Read about the lives of these two men and summarize the methods they used to help India gain its independence.

44

<u>OTHER IDEAS/NOTES:</u>

ASIA: CURRENT EVENTS

Use the space below to record the articles you have found or the news that you have heard during your study of Asia. Clip out the news articles and glue or paste them to a separate sheet of paper. Insert those pages after this page in your notebook.

Date of Newspaper or Radio/TV Broadcast	Name of Newspaper or News Station	Topic of News Item*
_____	_____	_____
_____	_____	_____
_____	_____	_____
_____	_____	_____
_____	_____	_____
_____	_____	_____
_____	_____	_____

* Examples: National currency, war, leadership, economics, government, environment, social issues, natural disasters (earthquakes, volcano eruptions)

EUROPE

RESOURCES

TEXTBOOKS

GRADE LEVEL	TITLE	AUTHOR/ PUBLISHER
4-6	*Old World History and Geography*	A Beka Book
7-12	*History of the World in Christian Perspective*	A Beka Book
7-12	*World Geography in Christian Perspective*	A Beka Book
7-12	*World Studies for Christian Schools*	Bob Jones Univ. Press
7-12	*Streams of Civilization*	Christian Liberty Press

BOOKS OF INTEREST/READERS

2nd up	*Pompeii: Buried Alive*	Kunhardt
4th up	*The Door in the Wall*	DeAngeli
4th up	*The Children's Homer*	Colun
5th up	*The Morning Star of the Reformation*	Thompson
5th up	*The Hiding Place*	Ten Boom
5th up	*Shadow of a Bull*	Wojciechowska
5th up	*The Trumpeter of Krakow*	Kelly
6h up	*The Hawk that Dare Not Hunt by Day*	O'Dell
6th up	*Otto of the Silver Hand*	Pyle
6th up	*Adam of the Road*	Vining
6th up	*Snow Treasure*	McSurigan
6th up	*Escape from Warsaw*	Serraillier
6th up	*Shadow of the Bull*	Wojciechowska
9th up	*A Tale of Two Cities*	Charles Dickens
9th up	*Hard Times*	Charles Dickens
9th up	*Julius Caesar*	Shakespeare

<u>MISSIONARIES AND OTHER PEOPLE YOU MAY WANT TO READ ABOUT</u>

Wilberforce	**Martin Luther**	**John Calvin**
Wycliffe	**John Tyndale**	**Alexander the Great**
Napoleon	**Hitler**	**Margaret Thatcher**

*Other musicians, artists, authors, and scientists are listed
at the end of the Culture section.*

EUROPE: GEOGRAPHY

Use an atlas, encyclopedia, textbooks, and/or library books to find answers to the following questions.

IDENTIFY:

1.   Europe's longest river -

2.   Europe's second longest river -

3.   the European country known as the "land of thousands of lakes" -

4.   the largest saltwater lake in the world -

5.   the major peninsulas that are part of Europe -

6.   the largest mountain system in Europe -

7.   the mountain range that divides Spain and France -

8.   the mountain range that is the major division between Asia and Europe -

9.   the city "set on seven hills" -

10.   the river which flows through Paris, France -

11.   the country known for its colorful **tulip fields** -

12.   the term which is used when referring to both Europe and Asia as one continent -

13.   the land of "fire and ice" -

14.   the home of Hans Christian Andersen -

15.　　the world's largest island -

16.　　Europe's highest mountain peak -

17.　　the location of the Matterhorn -

6

DEFINE:

1.   fjord -

2.   tundra -

3.   taiga -

GEOGRAPHY QUESTIONS:

1. What countries are included on the Balkan peninsula?

2. List three major islands located in the Mediterranean Sea.

3. Name two straits that run from the Mediterranean Sea.

4. What is the name of the highest mountain peak in Greece?

5. What is the name of the active volcano on Sicily's eastern coast?

6. Which mountains are called the "backbone of Italy"?

7. What is the principle river of England?

8. The Po River is which country's longest river?

9. Which European city was once separated by a wall?

10. In which city would you find the Cathedral of Notre Dame, the Eiffel Tower, and the Louvre Museum?

11. What major city would you find along the Thames River?

12. In which country would you find the Black Forest?

13. In which city would you find streets that were actually water canals?

14. Where are the sunny beaches called the **Riviera** located?

15. Name the mountains, the river, and the sea which form Europe's eastern boundary.

16. In which area of Europe are **fjords** found?

17. What countries are included in the Scandinavian peninsula?

18. What country is located on the Jutland peninsula?

19. What countries are part of the Iberian peninsula?

20.   Where is the Rock of Gibraltar located?

21.   Where are the White Cliffs of Dover?   Why are they so white?

22.   Italy has two independent states that lie within its borders. What are their names?

- NOTES -

MAP ACTIVITY. Trace a map of the continent of Europe. Label the following items.

Countries *(Capital Cities)*

___ Albania *(Tiranë)*
___ Armenia *(Yerevan)*
___ Azerbaijan *(Baku)*
___ Belgium *(Brussels)*
___ Bulgaria *(SofÍa)*
___ Czech Republic *(Prague)*
___ Estonia *(Tallinn)*
___ France *(Paris)*
___ Germany *(Berlin, Bonn)*
___ Greece *(Athens)*
___ Iceland *(Reykjavik)*
___ Italy *(Rome)*
___ Liechtenstein *(Vaduz)*
___ Luxembourg *(Luxembourg)*
___ Malta *(Valletta)*
___ Monaco *(Monaco)*
___ Norway *(Oslo)*
___ Portugal *(Lisbon)*
___ Russia *(Moscow)*
___ Slovakia *(Bratislava)*
___ Spain *(Madrid)*
___ Switzerland *(Bern)*
United Kingdom: ___ England *(London)*
               ___ N. Ireland *(Belfast)*
___ Serbia & Montenegro *(Belgrade)*
___ Corsica
___ Sardinia

___ Andora *(Andorra la Vella)*
___ Austria *(Vienna)*
___ Belarus *(Minsk)*
___ Bosnia and Herzegovina *(Sarajevo)*
___ Croatia *(Zagreb)*
___ Denmark *(Copenhagen)*
___ Finland *(Helsinki)*
___ Georgia *(Tbilisi)*
___ Gibraltar *(Gibraltar)*
___ Hungary *(Budapest)*
___ Ireland *(Dublin)*
___ Latvia *(Riga)*
___ Lithuania *(Vilnius)*
___ Macedonia *(Skopje)*
___ Moldova *(Kishinev)*
___ The Netherlands *(Amsterdam)*
___ Poland *(Warsaw)*
___ Romania *(Bucharest)*
___ San Marino *(San Marino)*
___ Slovenia *(Ljubljana)*
___ Sweden *(Stockholm)*
___ Ukraine *(Kiev)*
___ Wales *(Cardiff)*
___ Scotland *(Edinburgh)*
___ Balearic Island
___ Crete
___ Sicily

Oceans, Seas, Rivers, Gulfs, Straits

___ Atlantic Ocean
___ Black Sea
___ North Sea
___ Caspian Sea
___ Irish Sea
___ Danube River
___ Seine River
___ Thames River
___ English Channel

___ Mediterranean Sea
___ Aegean Sea
___ Adriatic Sea
___ Black Sea
___ Ionian Sea
___ Rhine River
___ Po River
___ Dnieper River
___ Strait of Gibraltar

___ Norwegian Sea
___ Bay of Biscay
___ Persian Gulf
___ Baltic Sea
___ Volga River
___ Oder River
___ Rhône River
___ Elbe River
___ the Dardanelles

Mountains

___ Alps Mountains
___ Ural Mountains
___ Caucasus Mountains

___ Pyrenees Mountains
___ Mt. Vesuvius

___ Apennines Mountains
___ Mt. Etna

GEOGRAPHY ACTIVITY SUGGESTIONS: EUROPE

1.   Memorize the capitals of several European countries.

2.   **[UE/JH]**   ☙Research one animal found in Europe. ✍ Write or give a report which tells about this animal's environment--where it lives, what it eats. Also, give the natural enemies of this animal and how it protects itself. How are the young cared for? When are they considered an adult? Add any other interesting information you find out. Draw or cut out a picture of this animal and add to your notebook. (LIFE SCIENCE)

3.   Study a product (land-use) map in an atlas. Notice how the map uses a symbol to represent the agricultural products or natural resources produced in a given area. Draw a map of the outline of Europe and make your own product map. ✎ Use your own symbols and make a key which explains what the symbols represent. Using colored pencils helps to make an attractive and readable map.

4.   Study the time zones of the earth. Choose two different cities from this continent. Then calculate what time it is in those cities at the time you are doing this project. [MATH]

5.   Europe contains some excellent agricultural land. Choose a country and find out what agricultural products are grown and exported. ✍ Write a brief report of your findings to include in your notebook. (Suggested countries: FRANCE, ITALY, SPAIN)

6.   Compare the latitude of Europe and North America. Are their climates similar or different? If different, how are they different and what contributes to this difference? Orally share the information with the rest of your family.

14

Other Ideas/Notes:

EUROPE: HISTORY

TERMS:

1.   helots -

2.   pedagogue -

3.   polis -

4.   barbarians -

5.   dictator -

6.   patrician -

7.   plebeian -

8.   gladiator -

9.   feudalism -

10.   Renaissance -

11.   Reformation -

STUDY QUESTIONS:

1. What were the two most influential early civilizations on the European continent?

2. During what time period did the Greeks attain the high point of their civilization?

3. What were the two most famous city-states of ancient Greece?

4. What great leader from Macedonia (a kingdom north of Greece) conquered Greece in the 300s BC and became the ruler of Europe's first great empire?

5. During what time period did the Roman civilization extend?

6. The Roman Empire enjoyed approximately 200 years of peace. What is the term for this period of the Early Roman civilization?

7. What great religion began during the height of the Roman Civilization in Palestine (an Asian country which was part of the Roman Empire)?

8.   There were many reasons for the fall of the Roman Empire, but the physical reason was the invasion by several barbarian tribes from the north. What were the names of some of these tribes?

9.   **[HS]** As mentioned in question #8, the Roman Empire fell because of outside attacks. However, history records that Rome really "fell from within". Briefly state what is meant by that statement.

10. As the Roman Empire began falling apart, it split into two separate sections. What were these two areas called? What was the capital city for each?

11. What is the time period called which begins with the fall of the Roman Empire and ends with the Reformation? (approximately AD 500 - AD 1500)

12. What sickness caused the death of almost a fourth of Europe's population during the 1300s?

13. As the feudal system of Europe declined, the individual nations began to take shape. What were the earliest nations to assume some form of power?

14. The Great Renaissance period took place at the end of the Middle Ages. How long did this period last?

15. In which country did the Renaissance begin?

16.   After what ancient cultures did the people of the Renaissance try to model themselves?

17.   What invention of the 1440s helped spread the ideas of the Renaissance throughout Europe?

18.   What was the first book printed on the new printing press?

~ NOTES ~

<u>Suggestions for Further Research on EUROPEAN History:</u>

1. **[JH/HS]** ✍ The following individuals lived during the classical Greek era. List each person's name on another sheet of paper; then locate information about each individual in an encyclopedia or world history text. Beside each name, give a brief description of his contribution to history.

Socrates	Archimedes	Pythagoras
Plato	Euclid	Aristarchus
Aristotle	Herodotus	Hippocrates
Homer		

2. Make a time line of the important historical events of this continent. Some points to include would be:

   - **Peak of Classical Greek civilization**
   - **Peak of the Roman empire**
   - **End of Roman Republic/Beginning of Roman Empire**
   - **Beginning of the Middle Ages**
   - **the Crusades**
   - **the Black Death** (killing one-fourth of Europe's population)
   - **the Renaissance** (begins in Italy)
   - **Christopher Columbus-- first European to reach New World**
   - **the Reformation**
   - **the French Revolution**
   - **the Industrial Revolution**
   - **World War I**
   - **the Russian Revolution**
   - **World War II**

3. List some of the contributions of the Greek and Roman civilizations to western culture. Include areas such as law, art, mathematics, literature, architecture, and drama.

4. **[JH]** ✆ Read about the Roman Empire in a history text or other reference book. Find out the names of the Roman dictators and make a list. Then next to each name, briefly explain why he was considered a "good" ruler or a "bad" ruler.

5.	**[HS]** ⚘ The principles of Roman law are the basis for many western European nations. The **Justinian Code** contains these principles. Research the heritage that Rome has given to the field of law. Compare and contrast what you learn with the American form of law as well as the civil law of other nations.

6.	**[HS]** What Latin words are still used today in the field of law and government? Make a list to add to your notebook.

7.	**[UE/JH]** ⚘ Read and find out as much as you can about the feudal system. What was life like in a castle? What were the jobs of the **serf** (peasant), the **lord**, the **knight**, and the **king**? ✍ Write a short report which includes the information you found.

8.	**[UE/JH]** ✂ Build a Lego® Block castle. Read first to find out what a typical castle looked like. How was it laid out? What was the "keep". When you finish, show your work to your family and explain all the sections of your castle. (Suggestion: Take a picture of your castle to put it in your notebook!)

9.	**[UE/JH]** ✏ Draw a floor diagram of the layout of a typical castle. Attach a report that lists the various parts of the castle and the purpose of each area. Share your diagram with the rest of your family and then place in your notebook.

10.	**[UE/JH]** ⚘ Read about the life of a medieval knight. What type of training did he have to go through to become a knight? What was his main job as part of a feudal community? Tell what you learn either in writing or orally.

11.	**[JH/HS]** ⚘ The **Magna Carta** is one of the most important documents in history. What is this document? When was it written? By whom and for whom? Why was it written? Where was it signed? What were the long-term results of this document? ✍ Research this topic and write a report to include in your notebook.

12.	**[JH/HS]** The invention of the printing press has been said to be the "greatest invention of all history". ✍ Write an essay supporting this statement.	[COMPOSITION]

13.	**[UE/JH]** 🕮 Read about the young girl of French history, Joan of Arc. Who was she? What did she do? What were the results of her actions? Tell the rest of your family what you learned about her.

14.	**[JH/HS]** 🕮✍ Find out what you can about the **Reconquista** that took place in Spain in the 1000s. Write a paragraph summary of this event in Europe's history to put in your notebook.

15.	**[JH/HS]** 🕮✍ King Ferdinand and Queen Isabella are best remembered for their support of Christopher Columbus' voyage to the New World. However, they are also less favorably remembered in history as the initiators of the **Spanish Inquisition.** Research this event and write a short paper to add to your notebook.

16.	🕮 Read about the history of Scotland and Wales and their fight for freedom. Read particularly about Sir William Wallace and Robert the Bruce. Give a summary of your research to your family.

17.	**[HS]** 🕮 The French Revolution is one of the bloodiest revolutions in history. After gathering the historical background of the situation, read **A Tale of Two Cities** by Charles Dickens. (There is also a video available that could be watched by <u>older</u> children.)	(LITERATURE)

18.	**[HS]** There has been a big political division as well as a cultural difference between Eastern Europe and Western Europe. What has contributed to this difference? Teach this information to your younger siblings.

Other Ideas/Notes:

EUROPE: RELIGION

DEFINE:

1.   martyr -

2.   catacomb -

3.   monastery -

4.   monk -

5.   pilgrimage -

6.   indulgence -

STUDY QUESTIONS:

1. Jesus Christ lived during the time of the great Roman Empire. It wasn't very long after his death, however, when it became a crime to be a "Christian". Who was the Roman emperor who declared it a crime to be a Christian?

2. How long did the persecution of Christians go on in the Roman Empire?

3. Which Roman emperor brought relief to the severe treatment Christians endured during this time?

4. During the Middle Ages, the Muslims had conquered the Middle East (the birthplace of Jesus). This angered the European Christians because they could no longer freely travel to the Holy Lands. What did they do to try to free Palestine from Muslim control?

5.   Who was John Wycliffe? What did he do? What is he often called?

6.   **[HS]** What is the Protestant Reformation?

[UE/JH] Who is responsible for beginning the Protestant Reformation movement?

- NOTES -

Suggestions for Further Research on the Religion of EUROPE:

1.   **[JH/HS]**   Read about the Crusades of the Middle Ages. Who called the people to action? Why were they fought? What were the names of the major crusades? What happened during the Children's Crusade? What was the result of the people's efforts? Was Jerusalem freed? What kinds of changes did the Crusades bring about to the European way of life?   Write a report to include in your notebook.

2.   **[JH/HS]**   Europe has many Christian heroes in its history. Look up the following people and explain their contribution to the Christian faith. Some of them had many followers. Tell what the group believed. Some were martyred. Explain why they were killed and how they were killed.

   Peter of Bruis (Petrobruscans)   **Peter Waldo** (Waldensians)
   John Wycliffe (Lollards)   **John Huss** (Hussites)
   Thomas à Kempis   **Johann Wessel**
   Erasmus

3.   **[HS]**   As the Protestant Reformation spread throughout Europe, many denominations formed from various teachings and beliefs. Research to find at least three of these original groups. Who was their leader? What did he teach? What modern churches have their roots in this early church? Give your findings in a report for your notebook.

Other Ideas/Notes:

EUROPE: CULTURE

As with any of the continents studied so far, the culture will vary with any given area. Europe is no different. Even though it is one of the smallest continents, it has a large number of separate and independent nations with different languages, different currencies, and different types of governments, etc. Another aspect to think about when studying the culture of this continent is the fact that we, as Americans, have received a lot of our nation's own culture, our way of life, from our European forefathers. Although the United States is indeed a type of "melting pot", it is still from Europe that we have received the largest portion of who we are as Americans.

So, for this section of study, this study guide will offer you a "quick quiz" so that you can check your own knowledge and understanding of some of the things that are quite "European". After taking the "quiz", go to your local library (preferably the children's section!) and browse through as many books on as many European countries as your study schedule will allow.

Here's the "QUIZ": Write down the European country that comes to mind when you read the following word or phrase:

1.   OPERA - _____

2.   PASTRIES - _____

3.   SAUERKRAUT - _____

4.   HAUTE CUISINE - _____

5.   WINDMILLS - _____

6.   RHAPSODIES - _____

7.   BAGPIPES - _____

8.   A LEANING TOWER - _____

9.   GYPSIES - _____

10. BULL FIGHTS - _____

11. TULIPS - _____

12. FASHION - _____

13. PIZZA, SPAGHETTI - _____

14. "THE SOUND OF MUSIC" -

     _____

15. OKTOBERFEST - _____

16. EIFFEL TOWER - _____

17. BIG BEN - _____

18. CHALETS - _____

19. "EL CID" - _____

20. RUGBY - _____

21. WOODEN SHOES - _____

22. FLAMENCO DANCERS - _____

23. NOTRE DAME - _____

24. ZEUS - _____

25. ST. PATRICK'S DAY - _____

26. KILTS - _____

27. BUCKINGHAM PALACE - _____

28. COLISEUM - _____ -

~NOTES~

<u>Suggestions for Further Research on the Culture of EUROPE:</u>

1.   **[UE]** The setting for many of the Grimm fairy tales is the Black Forest of Germany. Who is "Grimm" of these fairly tales? What are the names of some of the stories? 📖 Read one of these fairly tales and then design a book cover for the story. Be sure to add the title of the story on your book cover. Add this drawing to your notebook.

2.   Many of the world's greatest scientists, musicians, and artists have come from the continent of Europe. Several are listed below. Choose one of the following activities to do:

   📖 Read a biography. (Why not try one biography from each group!). Then write a short summary of this person's life to include in your notebook. Share something about this person's life with the rest of your family.

   📖 Choose three or more from each group. Look up each person to find their most important contribution/s to history. Make a list of what you find to add to your notebook.

scientists:	**Johann Kepler**
	Albert Einstein (later became an American citizen)
	Louis Pasteur
	Pierre and Marie Curie
	Galileo Galilei
	Michael Faraday
	Lord Kelvin

musicians:	**Johann Sebastian Bach**
	George Frederick Handel
	Ludwig van Beethoven
	Rimsky-Korsakov
	Tchaikovsky

artists:	**Rembrandt**	**Reubens**
	Van Gogh	**Michelangelo**
	Leonardo da Vinci	**Raphael**
	Verdi	**Puccini**
	El Greco	**Albrecht Dürer**
	Jan Van Eyck	**Lorenzo Ghiberti**

3. Several well-known authors also come from Europe. Look up the following people in an encyclopedia and list one or two of their most prominent works.

Hans Christian Andersen	**Miguel de Cervantes**
William Shakespeare	**Anton Chekhov**
Robert Browning	**Leo Tolstoy**
Charles Dickens	**Alexander Solzhenitsyen**
Rudyard Kipling	**John Bunyan**
Robert Louis Stevenson	**John Milton**
Daniel Defoe	**Johann Wyss**
Mary Mapes Dodge	**Johanna Spyri**

4. [UE/JH] Choose at least four countries from Europe and draw and color the flags of those countries. Use a separate sheet of paper for each country. Use the bottom half of the paper to list the nation's unit of currency, the current political leader, the type of government, and the capital city.

5. One can't think of Italy without thinking of pizza and spaghetti. Are they truly Italian dishes? Are they popular all over the country or are they regional dishes? Research the cuisine of Italy. After doing a thorough research, why not volunteer to prepare a meal for your family--complete with a report on what you've learned! (P. S. Be sure to serve some *antipasto!*)

6. Watch, or listen to, an Italian opera. Some preliminary study would probably make the listening more enjoyable and aid in one's understanding. What is the history of opera? Who have been some of the opera greats (both past and present)? Use the information you find to give a presentation to your family (with a sampling of the music included).

7. Occasionally on the news you may hear of someone having money in a Swiss bank account. Why are people interested in placing their money in a bank in Switzerland?

OTHER IDEAS/NOTES:

EUROPE: CURRENT EVENTS

Use the space below to record the articles you have found or the news that you have heard during your study of Europe. Clip out the news articles and glue or paste them to a separate sheet of paper. Insert those pages after this page in your notebook.

Date of Newspaper or Radio/TV Broadcast	Name of Newspaper or News Station	Topic of News Item*
_____	_____	_____
_____	_____	_____
_____	_____	_____
_____	_____	_____
_____	_____	_____
_____	_____	_____
_____	_____	_____

* Examples: National currency, war, leadership, economics, government, environment, social issues, natural disasters (earthquakes, volcano eruptions)

NORTH AMERICA

RESOURCES

TEXTBOOKS

GRADE LEVEL	TITLE	AUTHOR/ PUBLISHER
4-6	*New World History and Geography*	A Beka Book
4-6	*Heritage Studies, grade 5*	Bob Jones Univ. Press
4-9	*World History Series: Exploration & Discovery*	Usborne
4-9	*A History of US Book One: The First Americans*	Joy Hakim
7-12	*World Geography in Christian Perspective*	A Beka Book

READERS

3-up	*Leif the Lucky*	D'Aulaire
3-up	*Dakota Dugout*	Ann Turner
3-up	*The Light and the Glory for Children*	Peter Marshall
3-up	*Calico Captive*	Elizabeth Speare
4-up	*Tikta' Liktak*	Houston
5-up	*Streams to the River, River to the Sea*	Scott O'Dell
6-up	*Water Sky*	George
6-up	*The Light and the Glory*	Peter Marshall
7-up	*The Last of the Mohicans*	James F. Cooper

PEOPLE YOU MAY WANT TO READ ABOUT

Leif Ericson   **Christopher Columbus**   **Sir Wilfred Grenfell**

⇨ **Please Note:** Although Mexico and Central America are technically part of the North American continent, the study of this area is included with South America because of their cultural similarities.

North America: GEOGRAPHY

Use an atlas, encyclopedia, textbooks, and/or library books to find answers to the following questions.

IDENTIFY:

1.   the highest mountain in North America -

2.   the lowest place in North America -

3.   the world's largest fresh water lake -

4.   the world's largest island -

5.   the world's largest prairie -

6.   the only Great Lake located totally within the borders of the US -

7.   the largest national park in the US -

8.   the largest canyon in the world -

9.   the deepest canyon in the US -

10.   the deepest lake in the US -

11.   the highest peak in the continental US -

12.   North America's highest waterfalls -

13.   a famous geyser -

14.   the first English colony in North America -

15.   the first permanent colony in North America -

4

DEFINE:

1.   canal -

2.   iceberg -

3.   glacier -

4.   ice shelf -

5.   prairie -

6.   tumbleweed -

7.   tributary -

8.   hot spring -

9.   geyser -

GEOGRAPHY QUESTIONS:

1.   Where is North America's continental divide located?

2.   List three tributaries to the Mississippi River.

3.   List three deserts located in North America.

4.   Why are almost all the lakes in the Great Basin Desert region salty?

5.   Where is the world's tallest tree located? What kind of tree is it?

6.   What is the name of another very large tree that grows in the Sierra Nevada Range?

7.   What are some of Canada's natural resources?

8.   What are some of the natural resources of the United States?

9.   Name two animals that can only be found in North America.

10.   For what is the "General Sherman Tree" of Sequoia National Park famous?

11.   Give the name of the peninsula that extends south of the state of California.

12.   Where and what is the Piedmont Plateau?

13.   What famous ship sank in the North Atlantic Ocean after striking an iceberg?

NOTES

MAP ACTIVITY. Trace a map of the continent of North America. Label the following items.

Major Points of Geographic Interest *(Capital Cities)*

___ Canada *(Ottawa)*   ___ Nova Scotia *(Halifax)*   ___ Quebec *(Quebec)*
___ Alberta *(Edmonton)*   ___ Ontario *(Toronto)*   ___ Manitoba *(Winnipeg)*
___ Yukon *(Whitehorse)*   ___ Saskatchewan *(Regina)*
___ Newfoundland *(St. John's)*   ___ British Columbia *(Victoria)*
___ New Brunswick *(Fredericton)*
___ Northwest Territories *(Yellowknife)*   ___ United States *(Washington, D.C.)*
___ Prince Edward Island *(Charlottetown)*   ___ Alaska *(Juneau)*

Key Cities

___ Chicago   ___ New York   ___ San Francisco   ___ Los Angeles
___ Denver   ___ Miami   ___ Seattle   ___ Boston
___ New Orleans   ___ Indianapolis   ___ Dallas   ___ Atlanta
___ Phoenix   ___ Detroit   ___ Anchorage   ___ Montreal

Islands

___ Baffin Island   ___ Victoria Island   ___ Vancouver Island
___ Aleutian Islands   ___ Greenland [belongs to Denmark, but in western hemisphere)

Oceans, Seas, Rivers, Gulfs, Straits

___ Atlantic Ocean   ___ Pacific Ocean   ___ Hudson Bay

___ James Bay   ___ Hudson Strait   ___ Davis Strait

___ Baffin Bay   ___ Beaufort Sea   ___ Bay of Fundy

___ Foxe Basin   ___ Great Bear Lake   ___ Great Slave Lake

___ Lake Winnipeg   ___ Gulf of St. Lawrence   ___ St. Lawrence River

___ Sault Ste. Marie Canal   ___ Lake Superior   ___ Lake Michigan

___ Lake Huron   ___ Lake Erie   ___ Lake Ontario

___ Great Salt Lake   ___ Mississippi River   ___ Colorado River

___ Ohio River   ___ Rio Grande River   ___ Gulf of Mexico

___ Bering Strait   ___ Niagara Falls

Mountains, Deserts, and other features

___ Rocky Mountains   ___ Appalachian Mountains   ___ Cascade Mountains

___ Sierra Nevada Mtns.   ___ Adirondack Mtns.   ___ Grand Canyon

___ Ozark Mtns.   ___ Death Valley

GEOGRAPHY ACTIVITY SUGGESTIONS: North America

1.   Memorize the capitals of the Canadian provinces.

2.   Choose three of the "key cities" listed on the "Map Activity" page. Determine the latitude and longitude of each city. Record this information and place in your notebook.

3.   If you have not done so, memorize the capitals of the 50 United States.

Other Ideas/Notes:

NORTH AMERICA: HISTORY

<u>TERMS:</u>

1.   portage -

2.   galleon -

3.   privateer -

4.   colonies -

5.   mercantilism -

6.   sea dogs -

STUDY QUESTIONS:

1.   Why are the native Americans called "Indians"?

2.   List several native American Indian tribes of the North American continent and tell what area they were located in.

3.   Who were probably the first people to arrive on the North American continent?

4. Approximately when did these people arrive?

5. Who were the Vikings?

6. Who was the first man from <u>any</u> country (besides the Vikings) to land on the North American continent?

7. Who was trying to find the **Fountain of Youth**?

8. Who discovered the Grand Canyon?

9. What was he actually searching for when the Grand Canyon was found?

10. List the name of the ships that carried the following groups to the New World:

Christopher Columbus and his crew -

the Pilgrims -

the Jamestown settlers -

11. What two groups of people were aboard the *Mayflower*?

12. Who was the second Governor of Plymouth and what book did he write?

13. What document was sent by the American colonists to King George of England which listed the grievances they held against his leadership and that said they now considered themselves an independent country?

14. On what day was the above document signed by representatives from the 13 colonies?

15. How long had the United States been an independent nation when it found itself internally divided and at war with itself?

NOTES 🖉

Suggestions for Further Research on NORTH AMERICAN History:

1.   ☕ ✍ Listed below are three Indian chiefs who were involved in different battles. Research to find the conflict behind each battle as well as who the leader was for the other side. Write out what you find for a report or share the information orally with your family.

   Cochise   **Geronimo**   **Sitting Bull**

2.   Make a time line of the important historical events of this continent. Some points to include would be:

   - discovery of the New World by European explorers
   - Canada becomes an independent nation
   - United States becomes an independent nation
   - the American Civil War
   - World War I
   - World War II

3.   Find which states in the U.S. have Indian names. If you can, find the meanings of those names as well. Make a list to include in your notebook. You may want to include names of rivers and other landmarks as well.

4.   ☕ ✍ Canada has often had troubles throughout its history with unity among its people. Even in recent history, some groups in the province of Quebec were campaigning to have Quebec recognized as an independent country separate from the rest of Canada. Look for news articles about the movement and read them in light of Canada's British and French heritage. How did the trouble begin? How has it developed? What do you think is a workable solution? Use this topic to write an essay to include in your notebook.

5.   What is the relationship between Canada and the United States? If you were to travel to Canada, could you do so like you were traveling state to state in the United States? Or is there something else involved?

6.   🗐 During the Age of Exploration, the land and waterways of North America were explored, charted, and named by many European explorers. Make a chart which lists the explorer, the country each was from, and what he charted, explored, or named. Insert the chart in your notebook. The following explorers should be included:

John Cabot   Juan Rodrigues Cabrillo
Amerigo Vespucci   Vasco de Balboa
Juan Ponce de León   Hernando Cortés
Ferdinand Magellan   Jacques Cartier
Hernando de Soto   Francisco Coronado
Vasco da Gama   Sir Walter Raleigh
Francis Drake   John White
Champlain   Louis Joliet
Jacques Marquette

7.   A study of the Mound Builder Indians can easily be done in the Midwest. Near Evansville, Indiana, is an excellent museum of excavations and reconstruction of how these Indians lived. The area is called Angel Mounds State Historic Site. In Ohio on Route 73 is Serpent Mound located just northwest of Locust Grove. Also in Ohio is Mound City Group National Monument located north of Chillicothe on Route 104. Cahokia Mounds is just off Route 55 near Collinsville, Illinois.

8.   List all the wars that the United States has been involved in during its 200 years of existence. Briefly tell who each war was fought with and over what issue.

9.   Memorize all the Presidents of the United States in order of office.

10.   Compare and contrast the two types of governments of Canada and the United States.

Other Ideas/Notes:

NORTH AMERICA: RELIGION

DEFINE:

1.   Protestant -

STUDY QUESTIONS:

1.   What are the two largest religious groups in Canada?

2.   How was Christianity introduced to Canada?

3.   Who was the first foreign missionary <u>from</u> America?

4.   Name the prominent denomination of the circuit-riding preachers of the 1800s in the United States.

24

NOTES ✏️

Suggestions for Further Research on the Religion of NORTH AMERICA

1. ☙ Research some of the teachings of the Roman Catholic Church and find out what was being "protested" by the leaders of the Protestant Reformation.

2. Why did the Separatists want to "separate" from the Church of England? Find out about the disagreements they had with the English church.

3. ☙ ✍ Among the European settlers were some that worked as missionaries among the various Native American tribes. Listed below are a few of them. Read to find out something about at least two of them. Write a brief summary of their work and include any special contributions or accomplishments.

John Eliot	**Roger Williams**	**David Brainerd**
John Wesley	**Charles Wesley**	

4. What are the top ten Protestant churches in the United States? Choose two of them (which are different from your own church) to research. Compare and contrast their teachings with your church's teaching.

Other Ideas/Notes:

NORTH AMERICA: CULTURE

DEFINE:

1.   maize -

2.   mukluks -

3.   syllabary -

4.   adobe -

5.   wampum -

6.   potlatch -

STUDY QUESTIONS:

1. What does the word "Eskimo" literally mean?

2. What do the Eskimos call themselves?

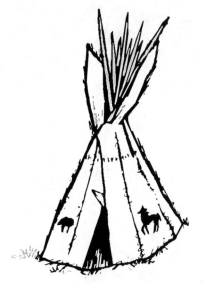

3. Not all Indians lived in teepees. Name some other types
    of Indian homes.

4. Which American Indian developed a syllabary for his tribe? Why did he do this?

5. What other language besides English is spoken in Canada? In what area?

NOTES

Suggestions for Further Research on the Culture of North America

1. 🎓 ✍ Listed below are several Native Americans who are remembered for some type of contribution or action. Find why they are remembered in history. List the ones you have researched and include their accomplishment/s. Add to your notebook after sharing with your family.

Joseph Brant	**Will Rogers**
Sequoya	**Massasoit**
Sacagawea	**Squanto**

2. 🎓 ✍ The life of the many Indian tribes varied not only from region to region, but also from tribe to tribe. Choose one tribe to research thoroughly. What did they live in? What did they eat? How did they travel? What ceremonies did they consider important? How did they dress? What kinds of art or music did they have? What games did the children play? After reading and researching this information, present what you have learned to your family. Be as creative as you can. You may want to build a replica of their home, their type of transportation, etc.

OTHER IDEAS/NOTES:

NORTH AMERICA: CURRENT EVENTS

Use the space below to record the articles you have found or the news that you have heard during your study of North America. Clip out the news articles and glue or paste them to a separate sheet of paper. Insert those pages after this page in your notebook.

Date of Newspaper or Radio/TV Broadcast	Name of Newspaper or News Station	Topic of News Item*
_____	_____	_____
_____	_____	_____
_____	_____	_____
_____	_____	_____
_____	_____	_____
_____	_____	_____
_____	_____	_____
_____	_____	_____
_____	_____	_____
_____	_____	_____
_____	_____	_____
_____	_____	_____

* Examples: National currency, war, leadership, economics, government, environment, social issues, natural disasters (earthquakes, volcano eruptions)